Melodic Falter

Clarissa Zhong

Presentation by *BookLeaf Publishing*

Web: www.bookleafpub.com

E-mail: info@bookleafpub.com

ISBN: 978-93-95755-46-7

First edition 2022

To those I love

Voicemail for Mother

My earliest memory is of falling
          asleep, with your arms around
me, a steady pat, pat, pat
on my shoulder that never seemed to exhaust
you.

Then I was counting traffic lights,
the grey blur of Shanghai outside our car
windows.
          Your white Toyota. The streetside pancake
shop
we love, waffle-thin with savory sweet
sauces; Chives and eggs and roasted oils.

Your many business trips. Your city office
in a tower of glass. Your fondness of jade and
          corals and karstic limestones, golden
ambers
and crystal amethysts. Your restlessness.
Your never-ending restlessness.

I felt distant from you. I could not
          remember the last time you hugged me.
The fights with Dad started in my earliest
memories and I couldn't understand the lack
of mutual love in the two faces I love;

I couldn't understand the coldness, the anger
of those warmest to me.

You took me to Europe the winter I was ten.
Stained glass windows and towering arches;
the rolling green of the Swiss countryside;
the dusty brown ombre of Galileo's lodgings,
        the pale slice of sky from which the first
telescope had seen moons, the moons of Jupiter.

I think you felt empty for most of your life.
There were dreams once,
        vague and safe and
tucked away in the folds of distant future as you
laid on the red mahogany floor of your
childhood
house, content & happy with your eyes
on the ceiling, half-sleeping.

Often I felt frustrated towards you.
And because you are kind
        I grew mean and
Bitter, disrespectful towards you as though
You had wronged me ten times in our previous
lives but
You had not.
        You did not deserve
My misplaced adolescent anger.

I bullied your patience, your good will because
        I couldn't bring myself to be loving,
to be fragile, to admit to myself that sometimes
I wish, I wish,
I could go back to that earliest memory
        of falling
asleep with your arms around
me, a steady pat, pat, pat
on my shoulder that never seemed to exhaust
you.

On a Good Day

On a good day you could memorise
the Lake.
The rolling green of the Swiss countryside
undulating under the shimmering sun.
    Awake.

Take in the blushful blue buoyant
on slumbering silver, a Glittering.
A calm
absent of self-sabotage, self-doubts,
the flickering feeling of – 'For how long?'

You feel uneasy in the moment,
pick up the phone to check the time:
2:46pm. You can stay here another 14
minuets and it's the 2-hour train back.
Uber? Bus? Your apartment.
Dinner. Shower. Work tomorrow.
Work the day after tomorrow.

You set an alarm. You breathe in, deeply,
bringing your attention back – you have to
memorise the Lake. The curling banks
bordering land and liquid.
    Lucid.

Metropolis of 1912

5

Excitement. It's burning in the air
That flew that rule that blew cheer hair
Hair that's fair, fair that's lair. Lairs
Of sights of smells of sounds of rare.

I am here. A note in my hand
And a name in my head. Feel of sand.

Eyes that shines and eyes that speaks. Eyes that
Speak and eyes that dream. Eyes that
Dream that scream: of clouds of light of clouds
of storm
Revolution roams. Past night past tomb.

Mortals

I often forget our mortality
        alive in the glimmer
        of a star
I often forget our worries
        alive in the tremor
        of a jar
How else could I have lived? Through
hazy mornings and languor years that sinks
into obscurity; memories forgotten as
the days danced into decades, debilitating,
disappearing.
How else could I have lived?

Sometimes I wonder if I should have chosen
to collect sunbeams and dream
dream up a way for more of us to be happy.
Limerence for lavish learnings
lemonade sundae, lyrical love songs.
Would I still have forgotten our

Mortality? The shadow that leans in as
We walk in the gloaming, the eucalyptus
a dim dark crimson.

Trade

Say,
Will you trade
Your shadow for
Another's?

Will you laugh
At the autonomy
Of a shape
Beyond
Command?

It could be
As still as
The ancient
Oak tree

It could be
As lively as
A bird of
Flight
Circling
The domain
Of your shadow

And even

Possibly
Probably
Very very likely
Surpassing

The confine of space

Will you watch
And perhaps
Befriend

Your shadow?

Will you read
Upon your
Deathbed
A deer
Cast upon the
Wall?

Who trot up
Closer and offers
A branch of wild berries
From her place
As you take
Your place
Amongst the
Stars.

Don't

Don't let your hands
off the wheels
Don't let the highway
Slip like bronze eels.

You're tired, you're numb
Eyes bloodshot denials
It's too fast, too long, too far
from the start
Grip loosens, loosened, losing all feels…

Why didn't you sleep? Why
Didn't you rest? Why did you
Drive on no stop – passing
Lake shops, cough drops?

Are you driving away
From the past? The silent town
And the slow mornings, the empty
Streets and the wind freezing,
The molten ground and that garden
Hose, curled around a crumbling
House, windows blistered.

Where are you driving towards?

A dot in the horizon today
and a petrol station the
Next, cut out images from
Movies, a hotel name on napkins
Dropped by a fur-coat. Thick accents
And orange fragrances – But you
Want an embrace.

Is there a need to keep driving?
You don't know but you know
You have to know, have to believe
You know, have to, have to,
Really have to—
Don't let your hands off the wheels.

Where do you want to go?
I pressed on, where are you
Really going have you given much
Thoughts—but the radio drowned
Me out, you had turned up the knob
And I asked on, voice raising and
Raising and raising—

And you let the wind in.
You rolled down all windows and
Nature roared in. Showing me
How useless it was to shout
At you, scream at you, when
You have to keep driving,

You have to keep driving or we'll crash,
We'll crash! Cars swore at you
And the wheels were burnt by the lines—
We'll crash! You shouted. We'll crash!
Tears running now, nose running.

We didn't roll the windows up.
We drove on. You did. You drove well.
The roads are never ending and always
Crowed. You can never be alone. Never
Be alone. I left you alone.

Snow is falling.

You have your hands
On the wheel, your foot on the
Pedals but you are not there.
Your mind had gone.
I gathered up the pieces,
Cotton soft with a fragile glow,
And I buried them in the glass of
The windows.

I braided your hair.
You did not speak and did not look at me.

Water Stains

Duck egg blue wrapped glass
—a jar, a once clean jar
Forgotten. What's it like to pass
No fuss, no blur air tar.

The stains of water
Dreamed a drummed
Rim, a melodic falter
That led to a neither – summed

Hear the fear
In her rushed breathing
Cascading notes down jeers
Re-lived, re-seen re-reading.
The sounds scrambled on keys
Softly, softly, be breathed.

Osmosis

I shaped you out of my loneliness.

Moulding lavender concrete,
Cinnamon sweet fancies,
Sunkissed copper glass glee,
A moss-covered melody.

When the moon rises you come alive.

I wonder if you could feel
My pain through my embrace.
I wonder if I could heal
My pain through your embrace.

Osmosis.

Our breathings mingle like a waltz
In slow motion.

I pondered
If I could tell you.

Only Dust Dances

Your features soften in sleep
the way snow melts in silent sunshine.

I blink and the memory is gone
        Only dust dances
On your side of the bed, prolonged
        Sparse space renounces,
Reorienting, your absence.

Your fragrance latches on
to the mid-noon breeze as it
        balloons out the linen curtains
daisy embroidered to match
your smile as we drove past the field
        of snow soft petals, a Saturday in July.

The Pineapple Man

Along hot buns and candy floss
Among egg wraps and chilli flops
Night and Day there stands –
The Pineapple Man.

He spins and peels and digs, gold
Disks and metal sharp risks, told
Roads and triple salt folds,
Rolling and rocking til old.

Hold! You hold the craved-out O, a fiddle
Plays afloat, one bite and no riddles
The sweet, the sour, the tang
Tingling and singling you drank

Streets change but not he,
We change and don't leave,
Ask him how what he sees
Ask him why what unease
He never had pineapples, never had he ate
The jade pale moonrise, far as the new East.
He pointed to his son, perched on a fruit truck
blue
With boxes as desk and streetlight as hue.
No hero true.

O Grand

There are mists over
Your brows, rover
Running ruins, rust-cover
Machineries. These used to hover.

You told me, these used to fly.
Discarded, left rotting, way past their height
Heavy, clumsy, they struck as poor sight
Slow, dumb, they reigned ruled old skies.

I wasn't there to see
Them. I wasn't there to see
You. You in your prime. Your youth. Tease
The boy in your eyes, still sparkling, and leave
Those hindrance of life, years building, of ease
Seeping, seeping, wrinkles creeping. Tough
readings.

As if we had walked past.
We met at the wrong part.
Met and not talked, smiles and sweet tarts,
Grandpa vs grandkid, three generations but our
hearts
The same stuff, for the same love, if our meeting
had last—

We would talk together, read together
Insulators, conductors, resistors and capacitors
We would laugh together, write together
Detectors, radiators, galvanometers
and—metaphors.

Then Ivory Sees Irony

Warmth. Cheeks tinted red with
Shame, laughed, screamed, ran and hid,
Footsteps echoed echoed echoed in
The dark, stilled, silence. A sin.

Keep your voice down. Do not wake
The dead, envious of life, of pity, faked
Oh hush, heartbeat, too loud, breathing
Stop, too stiff, too cold, too pale, unseeing

There, where moonlight meet, gilded frame,
Stolen sweet, scent of marble tamed

Renaissances. Silk silver swirls, spicy,
Then ivory sees irony, pure icy.

4pm Every Afternoon

4pm every afternoon raining or shining
        he comes to see her
bringing her favourite ceramic teacup, providing
cashews and almonds, dried apples and apricots
        a photo album or flowerpots
he comes to see her.

Here at the age care centre time slows and
pauses
almost stops. A common area with sofas, a
solitary
lady talking, always talking, fluent Italian
discourses
        on uncomprehending ears as she speaks
on, fragmentary
lines after lines her voice rising and falling and
never ending.

There are weekly movies – DVDs and a wall
projector
        The Titanic, an obscure musical, the
careful selection
Because so much trauma lives amongst the
residents

So fragile their frames, their minds, strong for
too long
And a silence too cruel, a history too close.

4pm every afternoon raining or shining
        he comes to see her
silent besides the talking lady and muted figures
        he holds her hand
the way forty years of love told him to hold her
        the way a life was built
far from their old country surviving the wind
and sand
of time—the discriminations and horrors
rampant in a land for dreams and ocean surfing
far, far from always summery.

4pm every afternoon raining or shining
        he comes to see her
She does not remember much and her eyes lose
focus but with him she still
        smiles, uncomprehending now
        as he holds her
        misty in his eyes.

Sunrise

Steam rising on battered sapphire
The shell of a car, motion void-
From evaporating perspire-
The dews delighting overnight

Languidly, lovingly, lavishly lost
    - a rose tint blooms sky full.

All is still.

Night is inches far and receding
Relenting—the unwillingness to let
Go, let be, let free
Let free.

The hold of the day that would not
End until the new day begins, the
Night that brings no tomorrow when
There is no end of today.

When you reach the scent
Of sunny dusted sea forms – I turned
By asking you,
Asking you when there's no answer
That's certain, no knowing of a

Future rented—

'Will you remember the gloom of solemn?'

Will you remember, I wonder, in the
Light of day—old solemn?

Dance in the Rain

At that moment I knew
You won't
Dance in the rain.
You won't
Drench to the core and
Throw your raincoat
Aside, all smiling in summer
All carefree.

Why should you?
Why risk a cold, a shirt
Ruined and mud in
Your shoes? All
Soaked and muddied,
Green smears of fresh leaves.

You smiled the invite away
You hold out an umbrella
Wide enough to
Obscure the dark sky,
The storm, the wind, the dirt,
The fear, the rage, the unhappy,
The unclear, unclean, the unknown

It's warm. It's safe. It's dry.

And I waved it away.
Convinced I didn't
Need it., or ever will.
Convinced I didn't need
You.
You who won't
Dance in the rain.

So I ran.
Down alleyways past shop fronts
Under bridges, glittering diamonds
And torrent of glass
Gleam of colours in
Downpour of grey
The world vivid
In motion in rain.

I danced in the rain.
And you lived from afar.
Busy in warmth and café glow,
The buzz of coffee flow.

I came in shivering,
Laughing, jabbering tales
Of wild and you
Embraced me.
Tucked me in toasted towels
While you drew me a bath.
You told me your stories

And you listened to
Mine. And at that moment

I knew: We are each
Happy, each in our lives.
Each living,
Each dancing,
In a place of our choosing.

At that moment I knew.

Love Loving

Thrill, the rush of air on a swing fall falling,
Tranquil, coffee cold, a neglect by chat chatters,
Dream, a temporal pause, to a CD spin spinning,
Melancholy, a grey tinge, in floral flat flatters.
Loneliness, a leaf, tore in tall torrents,
A face, faced by few faces how.

A sudden the sky goes dark, the town goes still.
Now

Thrill, the warmth, the morning sun on doorstep
stepping,
Tranquil, explosion, of thoughts in mind dance
dancing,
Dream, the world, health and rose-cheek
repping,
Melancholy, the ache, for many pain felt feel
feeling.
Loneliness, a hunger to comfort, of comfort, to
love, of love, love loving.

Scattered

I took out a compass to track the direction
The direction of clouds. Their speed in the
breeze
Delightful. Like almonds, like cream, a
perfection
Unhurried, unworried. They glide past pure ease.

I am seeking solace in wakefulness
Ill rested after the noise and clamours
Of dreams. The whispers of mad cruelty
Returning, invading, imploding.

Long shifts, for nerves on high alert
Who keep watch, who keep guard of my Absurd
That looms outside city walls,
That looms within my very core.

The same way that a shattered phone is handled
With less fear and less care
So is my shattered being handled
By me.
And by you—I hold dear.

A Castle of Fog

1

Look at me before words melt into sounds.
     Two trains colliding head on—
I see it in slow motion, ever so slow, the seconds
morphing
Into hours, the one image in layers that I could
     Walk through,
Shards comes first. Sparks glinting in the night
like
     Stars.
Or constellations in fatality. Then flyaway
Lumbers, rubbles, steel frames crumbled like
     papers, tissue thin.
Last the centre. Shrouded in smokes and flames
and anguish.
I dared not enter.
My heart, mangled by pain.
I dared not enter—
     I had to.

2

Build me a castle of fog, I said once

But it could be blown away, said you, it could fade with
A touch of sun, too heavy
Or a whispered word, too harsh.
All for nothing.
Or everything? I asked instead, for a castle of fog
is more delicate than silk or lace
more precious than gold
more vulnerable, unpredictable in the human hands
I will learn
to truly cherish
Every breath, every second, every blink
Where I exist.

3

The centre of the wreck is strange.
It's comforting, like a familiar terrain.
Missing roof, fallen walls, a jagged sympathy
Untuned.
I enter the driver's compartment and see no life
We know. But a life we think
we only know. Accelerating to ruin full speed
On a pre-laid track for we can't
Lose.
We can't lose.
Not to you.

I didn't know I had that much anger, that much
resentment
You heard what you wanted to hear, but not what
I said. Or what I wanted to say.
        I did the same and in that prolonged
instant—
Two trains collided.
And I see finally, beautifully, sorrowfully,
        My castle of fog.

The Rug, the Broom

Lucent sleep in picturesque aqua,
A fading shadow framed in ripples
Abashed with brume, perfumed, subdued.

You had left the telephone ringing,
The microwave spinning
The rug, the broom, all missing,
Our new beginning.

Turn back the jaded longings,
Nescient companions of noon.
Dug up music reformed, peel back
Poison performed.
Searching, searching,
For Logic buried in snowstorms,
For Reason carried in ghost forms.

We watched the procession of confessions
Repressed in grey slums of conceit.
We watched the obsession with aggression,
Impressed in stray blooms of concrete.

Velvet viridescent.
A healing of hypnotising hypocrisy.
Like ointment cool on

scars of geography.

The rug, the broom, all missing.
Our new beginning.

Setting

Soaked in the   comfort of semi-silence
There rose the smokes of   red incense
        Crawling, swaying, slowing, soothing,
Demanding forgiveness, begging fortunes,
ordering love.
A thousand hums silvering to scent
A single voice diluting to air.

Predictable, like temples on the top of mountains
Inevitable, like coins dreaming within fountains.
'A felicidade' plays like shimmering sunlight.

        I switch off the kettle.
I polish the glass.
I set the table.

Writing Poetry

Writing poetry is like reverse remembering,
Un-learning conceptions of lines,
Borders, shapes, senses, un-seeing,
un-burdening
The sounds, their textures, temperatures, times.

It's about letting dreams flow
Into reality, swirling symbols
And syllables, shadows and souls
All mingled…and where trembles
Are colours, correlations. Unconcern.

The words surrender their meaning,
Meanings. Layers of connotations,
Convolutions undressing; needing
A break from restraints.

Where logic falls back into a bath
Of sweet roses, softly scented
Souped spaces, a long
Exhale, the mists embracing.
Finally, when she is ready and rested,
She'd step out and reassesses.
The world spinning back into focus—
Recharged, revived, re-imagined.

www.ingramcontent.com/pod-product-compliance
Lightning Source LLC
La Vergne TN
LVHW010938200726
843509LV00013B/2240